by Iain Gray

Lang**Syne**

PUBLISHING

WRITING *to* REMEMBER

79 Main Street, Newtongrange,
Midlothian EH22 4NA
Tel: 0131 344 0414   Fax: 0845 075 6085
E-mail: info@lang-syne.co.uk
www.langsyneshop.co.uk

Design by Dorothy Meikle
Printed by Printwell Ltd
© Lang Syne Publishers Ltd 2016

ISBN 978-1-85217-670-9

Rees

MOTTO:

The hope of a better age.

CREST:

A lion rampant.

NAME variations include:
       Reece
       Reese
       Rhys
       Rice

Chapter one:

Origins of Welsh surnames

by Iain Gray

If you don't know where you came from, you won't know where you're going is a frequently quoted observation and one that has a particular resonance today when there has been a marked upsurge in interest in genealogy, with increasing numbers of people curious to trace their family roots.

Main sources for genealogical research include census returns and official records of births, marriages and deaths – and the key to unlocking the detail they contain is obviously a family surname, one that has been 'inherited' and passed from generation to generation.

No matter our station in life, we all have a surname – but it was not until about the middle of the fourteenth century that the practice of being identified by a particular, or 'fixed', surname became commonly established throughout the British Isles.

Previous to this, it was normal for a person to be identified through the use of only a forename.

Wales, however, known in the Welsh language as *Cymru*, is uniquely different – with the use of what are known as patronymic names continuing well into the fifteenth century and, in remote rural areas, up until the early nineteenth century.

Patronymic names are ones where a son takes his father's forename, or Christian name, as his surname.

Examples of patronymic names throughout the British Isles include 'Johnson', indicating 'son of John', while specifically in Scotland 'son of' was denoted by the prefix Mc or Mac – with 'MacDonald', for example, meaning 'son of Donald.'

Early Welsh law, known as *Cyfraith Hywel*, *The Law of Hywel*, introduced by Hywel the Good, who ruled from Prestatyn to Pembroke between 915 AD and 950 AD, stipulated that a person's name should indicate their ancestry – the name in effect being a type of 'family tree.'

This required the prefixes *ap* or *ab* – derived from *mab*, meaning 'son of' being placed before the person's baptismal name.

In the case of females, the suffixes *verch* or *ferch*, sometimes shortened to *vch* or *vz* would be attached to their Christian name to indicate 'daughter of.'

In some cases, rather than being known for

example as *Llewellyn ap Thomas – Llewellyn son of Thomas* – Llewellyn's name would incorporate an 'ancestral tree' going back much earlier than his father.

One source gives the example of *Llewellyn ap Thomas ap Dafydd ap Evan ap Owen ap John* – meaning *Llewellyn son of Thomas son of Dafydd son of Evan son of Owen son of John*.

This leads to great confusion, to say the least, when trying to trace a person's ancestry back to a particular family – with many people having the forenames, for example, of Llewellyn, Thomas, Owen or John.

The first Act of Union between Wales and England that took place in 1536 during the reign of Henry VIII required that all Welsh names be registered in an Anglicised form – with *Hywel*, for example, becoming Howell, or Powell, and *Gruffydd* becoming Griffiths.

An early historical example of this concerns William ap John Thomas, standard bearer to Henry VIII, who became William Jones.

In many cases – as in Davies and Williams – an s was simply added to the original patronymic name, while in other cases the prefix *ap* or *ab* was contracted to *p* or *b* to prefix the name – as in *ab Evan* to form Bevan and *ap Richard* to form Pritchard.

Other original Welsh surnames – such as Morgan, originally *Morcant* – derive from ancient Celtic sources, while others stem from a person's physical characteristics – as in *Gwyn* or *Wynne* a nickname for someone with fair hair, *Gough* or *Gooch* denoting someone with red hair or a ruddy complexion, *Gethin* indicating swarthy or ugly and *Lloyd* someone with brown or grey hair.

With many popular surnames found today in Wales being based on popular Christian names such as John, this means that what is known as the 'stock' or 'pool' of names is comparatively small compared to that of common surnames found in England, Scotland and Ireland.

This explains why, in a typical Welsh village or town with many bearers of a particular name not necessarily being related, they were differentiated by being known, for example, as 'Jones the butcher', 'Jones the teacher' and 'Jones the grocer.'

Another common practice, dating from about the nineteenth century, was to differentiate among families of the same name by prefixing it with the mother's surname or hyphenating the name.

The history of the origins and development of Welsh surnames is inextricably bound up with the nation's frequently turbulent history and its rich culture.

Speaking a Celtic language known as Brythonic, which would gradually evolve into Welsh, the natives were subjected to Roman invasion in 48 AD, and in the following centuries to invasion by the Anglo-Saxons, Vikings and Normans.

Under England's ruthless and ambitious Edward I, the nation was fortified with castles between 1276 and 1295 to keep the 'rebellious' natives in check – but this did not prevent a series of bloody uprisings against English rule that included, most notably, Owain Glyndŵr's rebellion in 1400.

Politically united with England through the first Act of Union in 1536, becoming part of the Kingdom of Great Britain in 1707 and part of the United Kingdom in 1801, it was in 1999 that *Cynulliad Cenedlaethol Cymru*, the National Assembly for Wales, was officially opened by the Queen.

Welsh language and literature has flourished throughout the nation's long history.

In what is known as the Heroic Age, early Welsh poets include the late sixth century Taliesin and Aneirin, author of *Y Gododdin*.

Discovered in a thirteenth century manuscript but thought to date from anywhere between the seventh and eleventh centuries, it refers to the kingdom of Gododdin that took in south-east Scotland and

Northumberland and was part of what was once the Welsh territory known as *Hen Ogledd*, *The Old North*.

Commemorating Gododdin warriors who were killed in battle against the Angles of Bernicia and Deira at Catraith in about 600 AD, the manuscript – known as *Llyfr Aneirin*, *Book of Aneirin* – is now in the precious care of Cardiff City Library.

Other important early works by Welsh poets include the fourteenth century *Red Book of Hergest*, now held in the Bodleian Library, Oxford, and the *White Book of Rhydderch*, kept in the National Library of Wales, Aberystwyth.

William Morgan's translation of the Bible into Welsh in 1588 is hailed as having played an important role in the advancement of the Welsh language, while in I885 Dan Isaac Davies founded the first Welsh language society.

It was in 1856 that Evan James and his son James James composed the rousing Welsh national anthem *Hen Wlad Fynhadad – Land of My Fathers*, while in the twentieth century the poet Dylan Thomas gained international fame and acclaim with poems such as *Under Milk Wood*.

The nation's proud cultural heritage is also celebrated through *Eisteddfod Genedlaethol Cymru*, the National Eisteddfod of Wales, the annual festival of music, literature and performance that is held across the nation and which traces its roots back to 1176 when Rhys ap Gruffyd, who ruled the territory of Deheubarth from 1155 to 1197, hosted a magnificent festival of poetry and song at his court in Cardigan.

The 2011 census for Wales unfortunately shows that the number of people able to speak the language has declined from 20.8% of the population of just under 3.1 million in 2001 to 19% – but overall the nation's proud culture, reflected in its surnames, still flourishes.

Many Welsh families proudly boast the heraldic device known as a Coat of Arms, as featured on our front cover.

The central motif of the Coat of Arms would originally have been what was borne on the shield of a warrior to distinguish himself from others on the battlefield.

Not featured on the Coat of Arms, but highlighted on page three, is the family motto and related crest – with the latter frequently different from the central motif.

Echoes of a far distant past can still be found in our surnames and they can be borne with pride in commemoration of our forebears.

Chapter two:

Fiery warriors

A name of Anglo-Saxon origin, derived as it is from the Old English personal name 'Rhys', or 'Ris', 'Rees' – meaning 'son of Rhys' – is of truly martial roots.

As a forename, and first appearing in the *Anglo-Saxon Chronicle* in the form of 'Hris', it indicated 'fiery warrior, or 'ardour.'

'Fiery warrior' is indeed an apt description, borne as it was by the eleventh century Welsh warrior king Rhys ap Tewdwr – and it was because of his inspiration as a freedom fighter that 'Rhys' became popularised as a surname.

It is also the forename from which the popular Welsh surname of 'Price' derives.

Recognised as having been the last ruler of Wales as an independent kingdom, Rhys ap Tewdwr boasted an illustrious pedigree, descended as he was from both Hywel Dda – Hywel the Good – referred to in *Chapter one*, and the famed Rhodri ap Merfyn, better known to posterity as Rhodri Mawr, or Rhodri the Great.

Born in about 820 and succeeding his father when he was aged 24 as King of Gwynedd, Rhodri came to control much of what is now modern-day Wales – to the extent that some sources refer to him as 'King of Wales.'

In what were particularly bloody times, he had to contend with both Saxon and Viking invasions – with the Vikings referred to by the Welsh as 'the black gentiles.'

The Welsh historical source known as the *Chronicle of the Princes* records Rhodri killing the Viking leader Gorm in 856 after the Norsemen had ravaged Anglesey.

Confusion surrounds the latter years of his kingship, with the chronicle stating that he was killed fighting the Vikings at 'the battle of Sunday' on Anglesey in 873, while other sources assert he was killed four years later along with his brother Gwriad in fierce battle with the Saxons.

His descendant Rhys ap Tewdwr took the throne of the area of South Wales then known as the Principality of Deheubarth – of which the modern-day county of Carmarthenshire once formed a part and with which bearers of the Rees name are particularly associated – in 1078.

But what was to eventually prove to be the death knell of Welsh independence was sounded in the wake of the Norman Conquest of England in 1066.

A key date in not only English but also Welsh history, by 1066 England had become a nation with several powerful competitors to the throne.

In what were extremely complex family, political and military machinations, the English monarch was Harold II, who had succeeded to the throne following the death of Edward the Confessor.

But his right to the throne was contested by two powerful competitors – his brother-in-law King Harold Hardrada of Norway, in alliance with Tostig, Harold II's brother, and Duke William II of Normandy.

On October 14, he encountered a mighty invasion force, led by William that had landed at Hastings, in East Sussex.

Harold drew up a strong defensive position, at the top of Senlac Hill, building a shield wall to repel his foe's cavalry and infantry.

The Normans suffered heavy losses, but through a combination of the deadly skill of their archers and the ferocious determination of their cavalry they eventually won the day.

Anglo-Saxon morale had collapsed on the battlefield as word spread through the ranks that Harold, the last of the Anglo-Saxon kings, had been killed.

William was declared King of England on December 25, and the complete subjugation of his

Anglo-Saxon subjects followed, with those Normans who had fought on his behalf rewarded with lands – a pattern that would be repeated in Wales.

Invading across the Welsh Marches, the borderland between England and Wales, the Normans relentlessly and ruthlessly consolidated their gains by building castles, for example in what they called 'Penfro' – later to lend its name to the town of Pembroke.

In 1081, Caradog ap Gruffydd, one of Rhys ap Tewdwr's rivals, invaded Deheubarth, forcing Rhys to seek sanctuary in St David's Cathedral.

But, forging an alliance with Gruffudd ap Cynan by pledging to aid him in his bid to regain the throne of the Kingdom of Gwynedd, Rhys was able to defeat Caradog at the battle of Mynydd.

It was in this same year of 1081 that William, victor of the battle of Hastings fifteen years earlier and now undisputed King of England, visited Deheubarth on what was purported to be a pilgrimage to St David's.

But no-one, least of all Rhys ap Tewdwr, was fooled as to the true purpose of his co-called pilgrimage – accompanied as he was by a battle-hardened host of ambitious and land-hungry Norman knights who by this date were more properly known as 'Anglo-Norman.'

Confronted with this daunting show of military might, Rhys had no option but to seek an accommodation with William by paying him homage in return for the right to keep his kingdom under the king's sufferance.

But it was an uneasy accommodation and matters came to a bloody head in April of 1093 when Rhys was defeated in battle at Brycheiniog – Brecon – by an Anglo-Norman force commanded by Bernard de Neufmarche.

Through time, as their grip on Wales tightened like a vice, these Anglo-Normans would become known as 'Cambro-Normans' – with 'Cambro' derived from the Latin term for Wales of 'Cambresis.'

Following the death in battle of his father, Rhys's son, Gruffydd ap Tewdwr, was allowed to retain a small portion of what had been the family lands.

Perhaps rather ironically, it is through this son that Rhys ap Tewdwr is recognised as an ancestor of the English Royal House of Tudor – with 'Tudor' an Anglicised form of 'Tewdwr.'

Rhys's daughter Nest, meanwhile, became the progenitor, through her marriage to Gerald de Windsor, the powerful Constable of Pembroke, of the mighty de Barry and FitzGerald dynasties of Ireland.

Welsh resistance to English dominance was brutally crushed in 1283 under Edward I, who ordered the building or repair of at least 17 castles and who in 1302 proclaimed his son and heir, the future Edward II, as Prince of Wales, a title known in Welsh as *Tywysog Cymru*.

But another heroic Welsh figure arose from 1400 to 1415 in the form of Owain Glyndŵr – the last native Welshman to be recognised by his devoted followers as *Tywysog Cymru*.

In what is known as The Welsh Revolt he achieved an early series of stunning victories against Henry IV and his successor Henry V – until mysteriously disappearing from the historical record after mounting an ambush in Brecon.

Some sources assert that he was either killed in the ambush or died a short time afterwards from wounds he received – but there is a persistent tradition that he survived and lived thereafter in anonymity, protected by loyal followers.

During the revolt, he had steadfastly refused offers of a Royal Pardon and – despite offers of hefty rewards for his capture – he was never betrayed.

Chapter three:

Politics and protest

Turbulence of a much different nature from that fomented through Anglo-Saxon, Viking and Norman invasion descended on Wales in the early years of the nineteenth century in the form of violent protests by rural communities against unfair taxation that was imposed despite a decline in agricultural markets.

Known as the Rebecca Riots, these protests – mainly throughout Cardiganshire, Carmarthenshire and Pembrokeshire – were in the main directed against the hated turnpike tolls that farmers had to contend with and also against rents, county rates and Church tithes.

It was in order to avoid being identified as they destroyed the turnpikes, or toll-gates, that the rioters blackened their faces and dressed in women's clothes.

This practice of disguising themselves had its roots in a form of 'mob justice' known as *Ceffyl Pren* – meaning 'wooden horse' – where offenders such as particularly harsh landlords or adulterers would be publicly humiliated by being berated and beaten while tied to a wooden horse.

In parts of rural Scotland and northern England,

meanwhile, the practice was known as 'Riding the Stang' – with offenders tied to a horizontal wooden pole.

In the case of the Rebecca Riots, the rioters – known in Welsh as *Merched Beca*, Rebecca's Daughters – are thought to have taken their name from the Biblical Genesis 24:60 that states:

And they blessed Rebekah and said unto her,
Thou art our sister, be thou the mother of thousands
of millions, and let thy seed possess the gate
of those who would hate them.

The first of the Rebecca Riots came in May of 1839 with the destruction of a new toll-gate at Yr Efail wen, Carmarthenshire, and led by a 30-year-old blacksmith, Thomas Rees, more familiarly known as Twm Carnabwth.

After the toll-gate was rebuilt, it was destroyed again the following month and the toll-house set ablaze.

Despite the best efforts of the authorities in the form of detachments of Yeomanry and the fact that Rees was actually rounded up and taken in chains to Haverfordwest jail, no-one was actually willing to name him as the leader of the Yr Efail wen attacks, and he was set free.

It was not until 1843 that the Rebecca Riots ended – as a result of the setting up of a Royal

Commission into toll roads and the subsequent Turnpikes Act of the following year.

The bold Thomas Rees, meanwhile, who became an inspiration in future years for other forms of protest, died in 1876, while his gravestone can be seen to this day at Bethel Chapel, Mynachlog-ddu, Pembrokeshire.

Involved in a rather more conventional form of social and political activism and in a later century, Merlyn Rees was the Welsh Labour Party politician and holder of high government office born in 1920 in Cilfynydd, near Pontypridd, Glamorgan.

Educated in England at Harrow Weald Grammar School, Harrow, and Goldsmith's College, London, he served as an RAF squadron leader during the Second World War and later studied at the London School of Economics.

A schoolmaster at his old school in Harrow from 1949 until 1960, it was in a by-election in 1963 that he entered full-time politics through his election as Labour MP for Leeds South – the constituency later renamed Marley and Leeds South.

He stepped down from the House of Commons in 1992, after having held posts that included Secretary of State for Northern Ireland, from 1974 until 1976, and as Home Secretary from 1976 to 1979.

Created a life peer as Baron Merlyn-Rees in the County of West Yorkshire and of Cilfynydd in the County of Mid Glamorgan, he died in 2006.

This was after having served out-with politics as president of the Video Standards Council and, from 1994 to 2002, as first chancellor of the University of Glamorgan, while Merlyn Rees Avenue in Morley is named in his honour.

One bearer of the Rees name with a particularly tragic claim to contemporary historical fame is Trevor Rees-Jones, also known as Trevor Rees, the bodyguard who was severely injured in the car crash in Paris in August of 1997 that claimed the lives of Diana, Princess of Wales, her companion Dodi Fayed and their driver Henri Paul.

Born in 1968 at Renteign, Germany, the son of a British Army surgeon, Rees-Jones was aged ten when he returned to his father's native home of Wales, settling near Oswestry.

Aged 19 when he enlisted in the 1st Battalion of the Parachute Regiment, it was some time after leaving the army that he was appointed as a bodyguard by the Egyptian-born entrepreneur and then owner of London's prestigious Harrods department store Mohamed Al-Fayed – charged with helping to provide security for his son and the princess.

While travelling from the exclusive Hôtel Ritz in Paris, owned by Al-Fayed, the vehicle carrying Rees-Jones, the princess, Dodi Fayed and Henri Paul was involved in a high speed crash in the city's Pont de l'Alma road tunnel.

A French investigation concluded that the accident had been caused by an intoxicated Henri Paul – Mohamed Al Fayed's security manager at the Ritz – losing control at the wheel.

Mohamed Al-Fayed, however, fuelled a number of conspiracy theories at the time by claiming the crash had been 'engineered' by Prince Philip – the divorced Diana's former father-in-law and the British security agency MI6.

In April of 2008, following a lengthy inquest into the accident in London, a jury found that it had been caused by Henri Paul's 'grossly negligent' driving, while the fact that the vehicle had been pursued by paparazzi had also been a contributory factor.

It was following this verdict that Mohamed Al-Fayed declared he was dropping his campaign to establish that the deaths had been by design, rather than by accident, stating that he did so for the sake of the late princess's two sons.

Trevor Rees-Jones, meanwhile, the only survivor of the crash, suffered injuries to his head that were so severe that his face had to be painstakingly reconstructed with the aid of family photographs.

Because of the traumatic injuries he received, he is still unable to recall details of the crash, but in 2000, with the help of ghost writer Moira Johnston, he authored *The Bodyguard's Story: Diana, the Crash, and the Sole Survivor*.

Chapter four:

On the world stage

Best known for his television roles of Lord John Marbury in the American political drama *The West Wing* and as Robin Colcord in the sitcom *Cheers*, Roger Rees is the award-winning Welsh-American actor and director born in 1944 in Aberystwyth.

Beginning his career with the Royal Shakespeare Company, he was the recipient in 1982 of a Tony Award and an Olivier Award for Best Actor in a Play for his title role in *The Life and Times of Nicholas Nickleby*, an Obie Award in 1992 for his performance in *The End of the Day* and a Tony Award nomination for Best Actor in a Play for his role in *Indiscretions*.

A naturalised American citizen since 1989, he also played the role from 2010 to 2011 of Gomez in the Broadway musical adaptation of television's *The Addams Family*.

In addition to *The West Wing* and *Cheers*, his other television credits include the British sitcom *Singles*, while his big screen credits include the 1993 Mel Brooks comedy *Robin Hood: Men in Tights* and, from 2006, *The Prestige*.

A Welsh actress of stage, television and screen,

Angharad Rees, later more formally known as Lady McAlpine, was born in 1949 in Edgeware, Middlesex.

The daughter of a Welsh psychiatrist, she was aged two when her family moved to Cardiff.

Following an education at the Sorbonne, Paris, the Rose Bruford Drama College in Kent and then the University of Madrid, she embarked on a stage career, acting in repertory theatre.

Her television debut came in 1968 in an adaptation of George Bernard Shaw's *Man and Superman* – but she is best known for her role from 1970 to 1975 of Demelza in the costume drama *Poldark*.

Her many other television credits include *The Way We Live Now*, *Doctor in the House*, *Within These Walls* and, from 1992, *Trainer*, while she was also noted for her role of Winston Churchill's daughter in the 1974 *The Gathering Storm*, with Richard Burton playing Churchill.

Big screen credits include the 1971 horror film *Hands of the Ripper* and, again starring beside Richard Burton and along with Elizabeth Taylor and Peter O'Toole, the acclaimed 1972 adaptation of Welsh poet Dylan Thomas's *Under Milk Wood*.

Other film credits include the 1980 *The Curse of King Tut's Tomb* and, from 1998, *The Wolves of Kromer*.

Founder of her own jewellery company, *Angharad*, based in London's Knightsbridge, she was married for a time to the actor Christopher Cazenove.

The couple divorced in 1994 and, following a relationship with the actor Alan Bates, in 2005 she married Sir David McAlpine, of the McAlpine construction group.

The recipient of a CBE and a Fellow of the Royal Welsh College of Music and Drama, she died in 2012.

In the creative world of the written word, **Matt Rees** is the award-winning Welsh journalist and author known for his *The Palestine Quartet* series of novels – the first of which, *The Bethlehem Murders*, was the winner in 2008 of the Crime Writers Association's John Creasey New Blood Dagger.

Born in 1967 in Newport, as a journalist he has covered the Middle East for both *Newsweek* magazine and the *Scotsman* newspaper, while from 2000 to 2006 he was bureau chief for *TIME* magazine.

Writing mainly for young adults, **Celia Rees** is the English author born in 1949 in Solihull, West Midlands.

A former school teacher, her novels include the 1993 thriller *Every Step You Take* and the 1996 vampire novel *Blood Sinister*.

In the genre of historical fiction, her 2000 *Witch Child* was shortlisted for the *Guardian* Children's Fiction Prize, while her 2003 *Pirates!* was shortlisted for the W.H. Smith Book Award.

A member of the Society of Authors and a former chair of the Children's Writers and Illustrators Group, her novels have been translated into 28 languages.

Serving as editor of *The Times* newspaper from 1967 until 1981, **William-Rees Mogg**, more formally known as Baron Rees-Mogg, was born in 1928 in Bristol.

Educated at Balliol College, Oxford and president of the Oxford Union in 1951, he began his career in journalism a year later with the *Financial Times*, rising to become assistant editor six years later.

Also active in politics, he unsuccessfully stood as the Conservative candidate for Chester-Le-Street in a 1956 by-election.

Moving to the *Sunday Times* in 1960, later becoming its deputy editor, he was appointed editor of *The Times* seven years later – one of his first editorials being a criticism on what he perceived as the severity of imposing a custodial sentence on Rolling Stone Mick Jagger for a drugs offence.

He wrote: "Who breaks a butterfly on a wheel?"

Replaced as editor in 1981 by Harold Evans after the newspaper became part of Rupert Murdoch's media empire, he later worked for a time as a columnist for the *Independent*.

Re-joining *The Times* in 1992 as a columnist, and having been made a life peer four years earlier, he was also chairman for a time of the Arts Council of Great Britain and vice-chairman of the BBC; he died in 2012.

He was the father of the freelance journalist **Annunziata Glanville**, born in 1979. Editor of the *European Journal* and a former leader writer for the *Daily Telegraph*, she is the sister of the Conservative Party politician **Jacob Rees-Mogg**.

Born in 1969 and a former president of the Oxford University Conservative Association, he was elected MP for North East Somerset in 2010.

In the sciences, **Sir David "Dai" Rees** is the British retired biochemist and science administrator who, from 1987 to 1996, served as chief executive of the Medical Research Council.

Born in 1936 in Silloth, Cumberland but educated in Wales, including at University College of North Wales, Bangor, he later was a lecturer in chemistry at Edinburgh University, specialising in the conformation and structure of carbonhydrate, before being appointed principal scientist for consumer goods company Unilever.

A Fellow of the Royal Society, president of the

European Science Foundation between 1994 and 1999 and a recipient of the Carbohydrate Chemistry Award by the Chemical Society and the Biochemical Society's Colworth Medal, in 2010 he became one of the 58 founding fathers of the Learned Society of Wales.

Reaching for the heavens, **Martin Rees**, more formally known as Baron Rees of Ludlow, is the British astrophysicist and cosmologist who has served in the prestigious post of Astronomer Royal since 1995.

Born in York in 1942, he is recognised for his important contribution to the understanding of cosmic microwave background radiation.

A former president of the Royal Astronomical Society and president from 2005 to 2010 of the Royal Society, he is the author of a number of popular books on science and astronomy – with his 2010 Reith Lecture for the BBC published as *From Here to Infinity: Scientific Horizons*.

From the sciences to the colourful world of art, **Lloyd Frederick Rees** was the distinguished Australian landscape painter born in 1895 in Brisbane, Queensland.

Of Australian, Cornish and Mauritian descent, he began work as a commercial artist in 1917 after studying at his home city's Central Technical College.

Later concentrating on landscapes, with critics noting how they depict the effects of light and emphasise the harmony between man and nature, he was the recipient of Australia's Wynne Prize for excellence in art in both 1950 and 1982.

An art teacher at Sydney University's faculty of architecture his many other honours and awards include Companion of the Order of Australia (AC) – the nation's highest civilian honour – and appointment as a Companion of the Order of St Michael and St George (CMG).

He died in 1988, the same year in which he was named one of the Australian Bicentennial Authority's "Two hundred people who have made Australia great."

Bearers of the Rees name have also excelled in the highly competitive world of sport – not least in the Welsh national game of rugby.

Born in 1858 in Tonn, Llandovery, Carmarthenshire, **Theophilus Rees** was the Welsh rugby union forward who was capped for his nation in the very first international match.

This was in February of 1881 in a friendly against England – with the latter crushing the Welsh by scoring thirteen tries in total and eight goals, with Wales unable to score.

It was in the following month that the Welsh Rugby Union was first formed.

Educated at Jesus College, Oxford and

appointed town clerk for the former Merthyr Urban District Council in 1905, Rees, who died in 1932, had played for the South Wales Football Club.

Born in 1910 in Swansea, **John Rees** was the Welsh international rugby union player who won fourteen caps.

Having played for Cambridge University, Swansea and, while working for a time at Fettes College, Edinburgh, for Edinburgh Wanderers, he died in 1991.

At the time of writing the most capped hooker for the Wales national team – with 61 caps – **Matthew Rees**, born in 1980 in Tonyrefail, South Glamorgan is the rugby union footballer who has played for teams that include Pontypridd, the former Celtic Warriors, the Scarlets and the Cardiff Blues.

Nicknamed "Billy Whizz" after the *Beano* comic character of the name because of his speed on the pitch, **Clive Rees**, born in Singapore in 1951 and also known as **Fred Rees**, is the Welsh former international rugby union player who won thirteen caps between 1973 and 1983.

Taking up rugby at Llanelli Grammar School, where he also proved to be a talented athlete, he later played club rugby for Llanelli.

From rugby to golf, **David Rees**, born in 1913 in Fontegary, near Barry, Vale of Glamorgan, was the gifted player who captained the Great Britain Ryder Cup team to victory over the United States at Lindrick Golf Club, Yorkshire, in 1957.

Beginning his golfing career when aged 16 as an assistant professional to his father at Aberdare Golf Club, he went on to win two British Masters, the South African Professional Golf Association (PGA) Championship and the Irish, Swiss and Belgian Opens.

Honoured as BBC Sports Personality of the Year in 1957 and the recipient of a CBE, he died in 1983.

This was after being involved in a car crash as he returned from watching an Arsenal football match – having loyally supported the club for a number of years.

On the football pitch, **Jason Rees**, born in 1969 in Aberdare, is the Welsh former international player who played for teams that include Luton Town, Portsmouth and Exeter.

From football to darts, **Leighton Rees** has the distinction of having been the first ever World Darts Champion.

Born in 1940 in the village of Ynysybwl, Glamorgan, he did not shine academically, with one of his teachers stating on his report card that he would be "good only for reading the sports pages of the *South Wales Echo*."

Confounding his teacher's lowly expectations

of him, he became a professional darts player in 1976 –
a career that culminated two years later when he
won the inaugural Embassy World Professional Darts
Championship in Nottingham, beating England's John
Lowe in the final.

Author of the 1979 *On Darts*, an auto-
biographical account of his life and times that includes
tips on how to play the game, he died in 2003.